The Fall P

By

Leisa Pierce

Table of Contents

Dedication i

Acknowledgments.. ii

About the Author iii

Dedication

This book of poems is dedicated to Rob, Michael, and Melanie.

They are the backbone of my existence.

Acknowledgments

First, I need to thank Rob Pierce, my husband, for his continued support, friendship, and this book's cover art.

I am grateful for my children, Michael and Melanie, who are now adults and continue to make me laugh. I am not only happy but extremely proud to be their mom. They are, without a doubt, the best gifts I have ever been given. I am delighted to welcome my new son-in-law, Sean, into the family.

I am thankful for my two siblings, who are still among us, Mary and Jackie and my brother-in-law, Jack. Since my first book, Moonstorms, was published in 2001, I lost my brother, Jerry, in 2008 and my sister, Pat, in 2018. My other brother, Jimmy, passed away in 1998.

I lost my mom in 2007, who always believed in me and was a great deal of inspiration throughout my life. She taught me strength and resourcefulness just by observing her life.

About the Author

Leisa Pierce is a Seattle transplant. Since beginning to assemble this book in 2006, she fulfilled a lifelong dream of returning to New England. After three harsh winters in New Hampshire, she retreated to her beloved San Diego in the Spring of 2014. Unable to find a sustainable income, she moved to Seattle.

Leisa has been writing since age 8. Her books include: "Moonstorms", "Midrange", a chapbook published by Maverick Duck Press in April 2007. Collaborations include a collection of poetry, "Sword Dancing", a collection of poems written with Vincent G. Novo, a contributing poet to "Poetry Has Had Its Way With Me", and several chapbooks.

Leisa's poetry has been published in Liquid Muse Quarterly, Comrades, The Writer's Hood, Born Magazine, Identity Theory, Wild Child Magazine, Sol Magazine, Purple Tights, Fluid Ink Press, Thunder Sandwich, Retort Magazine, NYC Poetry, Reader's Quarterly, Pegasus, THISPoets Magazine, Dream International Quarterly and Poetry and Insomnia.

The poems in this book were written in the fall of 2000, 2001, and 2002. Like Moonstorms, a good majority of her poems are written from dreams.

October
November
December
2000

Winter Scrapes

Winter scrapes
into a solitary,
slow easing.

~~~~~~~

Muse, Lend Me A Word

One tangled harsh word
leads the crew through
the rough
and dead seas.
Slough without an oar;
no ears to hear the needy.

Something about
pheromones
leaking out
with only a
band-aid to keep
still the steady drip.

Submerse yourself
in the work,
see if some float
toward you.

There are dead cats
strewn from
Heaven to Hell
in one's vision,
within sight of
subliminal surrender.

I've been here too
long, waiting
spring to find
new threads
to bear fruit on trees
that have no frost.

~~~~~~

Diversionary

Altered tactics
to dwell on, delve in to.
It's all tactile, and fingers
in the imaginary
swirls of the mind,
pretend brain swell.

Hold asunder
sudden desire
to roam
within the landscape;
refreshing recovery.

New obsession,
takes no possession
of body or spirit,
spoils the riches;
tames the famed.

I could fall here,
over this low balcony
into frothy mines.

I see diamonds
take shape
under water
as though this were all part
of some master plan.

A puppet to hold,
a pulpit to cover
sins of the want.

~~~~~~

Sip Slowly

I often miss
the trees
for the forest

in writing;
in love.

Tell me of your
dark shores,
I'll show you
my battle scars.

Lean on this
wisdom;
the years have
made me

well;
to listen.

Your spirit there
fired in red,
soothed in blue

take riddled
words;
hide the emotion

feign
over
reign.

You want to
drink of my
waters;

filtered
with
fatigue

the same
worry;
warrior
of a sky
mismanaged.

I want to sip
slowly
as this passes
before my eyes,

and not miss a thing.

~~~~~~

I Take

I take the morning
at the beach
with the kids
to build dreams
in the sand,
let the sun
wash over
stray thoughts,
carry me far
into the mist.

I take
the guilt and shame
for spending
my words
and it's Sunday;
day of redemption
and forgiveness.

I take a breath
and taste the salt air
that covers this skin
while they build
Noah's Ark
in the sand.

I take my time
to finish chores,
left undone
and watch teal
shades at the end
of the ocean
where the blue grey
meets the water.

I take shards
of memories,
drink them down
with a blue bottle
of ginseng tea.

I take this white wave,
open a new vein
and learn the act
of trust all over again.

~~~~~~

None To Be Found

I should walk the shore;
search for seashells
that take me back
to childhood
on the east coast.
None alike to be found
on a western front.
The empty
seawall stares back.
It's October
and the beach is sparse;
I like it this way.
My pink house
is just over my left,
the one I didn't get to buy.
There's a gathering
of people just below,
all ages, some kind
of reunion,
those two cute
blond surfers
steal a glance
at my cleavage as
they walk by.
One looks back
a little longer
than he should.
Inside, I smile
like a little girl
who breaks too
easy.
And the silence
of years suddenly
swell over,
spill into this.

~~~~~~

Manipulating The Landscape

Words escape as I rise
to breathe cool air.
Falling season
brings what it will.

I am reminded of
a cold November
morning in Nashville,
reading Frost under
the heavy quilt
Grandma left us.

He would get up,
make coffee,
leave me in bed
with warm memories
of the night before,
recite Poe
in the afternoon
over a beer and taco
at the corner shop.

He'd hustle grocery money
but we were never hungry.

He taught me
all I needed
to survive the streets,
how to shoot
a decent stick,
how to break
a heart.

I, so young
and full of ideals;
out to change the
world, the patterns
we grew out of.

He taught me
how to change
the spark plugs
on my Volvo;
how to ride.

Those days,
so long ago
yet something
stirs the wind,
I am taken back
to the years
when all we had
was today,
tomorrow's dreams;
yesterday never mattered.

Brilliant mind,
shattered
on midnight's fracture.

I look back
over my shoulder,
the times
that brought me
here
and I have to stop,
be grateful
for all the little
things he showed
me, like the path
less traveled
and how to break.

~~~~~~~

Falling In

Fall in to
the quiet lull
of early afternoon,
coffee scent
breathes smoke.
Memorize shadows
from a dream that is
almost forgotten.

Fall into the arms
of a lover,
Body scent
breathes passion.
Mesmerize eyes
that follow the dowel
on the page
like subtitles.

Fall in line
with the rest,
who quietly steal
the shallow breath
of poets and dreamers
as they read the news
of the day.

Fall in,
such a strange sight,
feeling the hand of God
upon your shoulder,
steer without din,
steely inside eyes.

~~~~~~~

I Don't Want To Play

I don't want to play counsel
and what have I done?

Build a wall,
only to fall
flat in the lap
of ghosts who ride
freely over the flesh.

We are not gods here
pretending the royal majesty's
circle of crowns.

Mere humans
who tinker away;
the words as time creeps
into dreams;
show big clocks
how to be maintained.

13 sounds like
a lucky number
to stop a dime on.
Stop the bleeding
before night takes
the skin under
the marrow.

Tiny frame,
a skeleton
of frail images.
This seems like
a good time to
say goodbye.

~~~~~~~

Cerebral Discussions

The bloodline
speaks clearly
of a time when
bishops and pawns
dined together
in joyous merriment,
in celebration of
cerebral discussions.

~~~~~~~

wheels

lumbering under
heavily wooded oaks
falling
falling

earth to moon
moon to sun
sun to water
and water
into
air.

this crest,

this wave,

this smooth

line finish
to nowhere.

balancing acts
of kindness
under breath
of taken women

into arms of battle.

find me
find me

dancing on
someone else's
moon,

someone else's
trace of language

where words
are broken

into meters

and meters
in to

rhyme
where no one holds
time as a weapon
and there is no
space
for hurt.

~~~~~~~

Tinge

Light the path,
fire the incense.
Smoke this flame
under winter ice;
weighted with cerise.
Storm the hills;
lay down
beside me.
Hushes carry
warm wishes
to spring.

Live the path,
tame the burning.
Torch this cinder
over summer heat;
made with amber.
Rain over th ocean;
walk with me.
Silent screams
torment until
the fall.

~~~~~~

hanging flowers

it's cold in here,
still, as life has
been in the past

driven hard
and long ago

blood shatters
soiled spirits
making rain
into thick
heavy dust

no one can
hear
from this distance
no one can
see
from the frozen
barrier

we leave up

humanely
hanging
flowers
around

~~~~~~

FirePlay

One: Under The Influence Of Fire

He thought
I was driving
while mainlining
and I am only
under the influence
of fire.

He needs to be
a confessor,
dressed in frosted glory
as the sullen
ashes tumble
with winter.

He can't see me here,
I hide in this invisible
realm, show
only hints of hues
when called upon.

I look back now and see
alliances and alike
in balance.

I love how this
inspires so deep,
swelling emotions
I keep spilling easy
on this anemic
night that holds
no sleep.

Two: Filler

She's looking like a confessor.

Reddish 12 hour lipstick
wears well against ruddy tones.
Inside, the rain destroys an aging face.

She's looking for an out.

There's nothing charming
in repeating
"Shut the fuck up!"

He's confessing
on a deathbed,
waiting for liquid end.

Sudden remorse
finds odd moments.

This is the day
it rains frogs.

Lining up the white;
true face of disdain
found its way
from early onset

of life.

Regret comes too late.
It rains in buckets.

Remorse for the shame.

Five drops to death.
Some just aren't strong
enough to see it through.

Sealed in a dirty room,
sucking up the snow
with red overtones
shining on an empty face.

It never stops
and there is no wisdom.

Final breath takes
us all,
there comes a blue wave
when we surrender.

Funny how life
doesn't play out
the way we think;
plan in the beginning.

~~~~~~

This Is The Wonder

And I am so alive today.
This may be the most
wondrous moment
in my life.

Look at the way the wind
blows the top of white caps
making spray that dances
over the grey.

These birds, they come
perch right next to us
on the wall, they talk;
birdspeak.

Watch them soar,
I wish I was a bird
for just five minutes.

This is Heaven.

This one bird,
accompanied by two
has only one leg.
He stands on the
flat of the wall, looking
straight into my eyes
and through me.

"But you don't need
legs to fly."

He takes off.

What wonder has
given!

21

My son tells me
there's a grey cloud
looming at the end
of the pier,
but nothing can
rain on this
perfect moment.

My daughter,
as we leave
turns to tell me,
"I can see the palm
trees in your eyes."

~~~~~~

Act Two

Man, I'm full of fire
and ready to burn.
I don't want a life
raft, I'm drowning
here and I love it.

Woman, slow down
you're gonna crash
fast and hard
and those little
blue pills are fading.

Man, I'm on the edge,
stand waiting to soar;
take me closer, take me closer
Hold me here; one final
kiss before I jump.

Woman, it's coming,
it's coming faster
harder than you thought
and ahhhh, the dreams
turn to pink ash whispers.

~~~~~~

Forbidden By Three

Taking fire to new depths
this sinking water climbs
heights forbidden by man.

This is it, this is it

And when the lights
come up, hold your
breath and soar.

This is it, this is it

I'm hitting; I'm running
and I ain't turning back
Slam, slam ouch, man,
take it back.

This is it, this is it

I'm everybody's angel
but no saving grace
tear into me,
take a slice.

This is it, this is it!

~~~~~~

Doesn't Fade

It's a slow burning comet,
one that doesn't fade
and I'm not sure
you ever understood
the full scope of this.

My skin crawls
with a chill now
that I've left the bed
where I left his warm,
tender voice.

Do you like watching
my sanity unwind?
As long as it isn't yours
it's like watching
a bad train wreck;
San Onofre's fault.

And I remember
that night well,
unfounded fear,
funny how one
leads to another;
unending battles
we soar under
pressure
but could never
find the foundation
to make a life.

It's never over
and you were
never a comet;
slow burning
star that falls

at every twist
and bend.
Flexing isn't
in your flesh
to any degree
I could live with.

Are you surprised
still I read so well?
The little nuances
left like breadcrumbs
on a broken path.
But, hey!
These roads are
scattered and different
and I remember well
the top of the mountain;
the trek there
can't be the same.
It is only time
and paths we choose.

You know
there will always be
a golden, esteemed room
that remains,
there are just some doors
I can't open it anymore.

I'll meet you
at the top
and I won't
forget a single
dream, a single
lesson; the scriptures,
shared moments
concealed like
fragile wounds
and I'll not
betray a single word.

And in the gold
of morning,
embrace the white
wave;
it's coming with
a closing photograph
that is burned in
my soul like harbor eyes.

~~~~~~

Something Has Broken

One

It's nearly two
by you and
something
has broken here
I don't know
what was so
fragile in
the early hours

breathe
exhale

inhale fire;
wish upon
a sapphire star

and in the not
knowing;
come morning
wait to see
what diamonds
are made of,
what strength
is gleamed
as bones creak
in the cold
of light

breathe
inhale

exhale water;
it brings shelter
from wind and
flame that is green

Topaz rising
under blanket
of fractured
wish

Two

These words we
spoke through
connected
hands;
did they mean
so little
for you to hold
in the dark
fading faith?

Three

Sleep, sleep
call from
somewhere
broken
deep inside;
a space
I cannot easily
visit

and I don't know
if I have enough
pretty pills to
satisfy what this
body has come
to need

Need, nothing
more than
inverted want

Want no more
than twisted
desire

I thought
we were alike
in ways
unparalleled

Four

Something
broke here
while my
head was turned
and I don't
know where to
find this missing
piece to make
it whole
anymore.

~~~~~~

Hemorrhage

One: That Place

It's only bad
escaping
that place that's
so hard to reach

I hurt just left of nowhere
where it ravels
the thread of spirit

The sleep was not
enough to replenish
any thoughts I may
have had underwater

A friend once told me
I will never drown
I try to find truth
when nothing seems real

The children nitpick
like true little artistes
and I haven't the strength
to stop

Just spin, spin, baby, spin
out of skeleton dust
crestfallen into the vast sea

It's all metaphors
and black;
this slow creeping

31

Charred from another life;
I can't see that far back
A broken spirit
but I didn't break it

There are some we never touch,
it is knowing when to stop
reaching;

unplug

~~~

Two: Never Too Young

I watch these children;
they dance
fragile hearts
learning the art.

I see my daughter;
the way she looks
at him, this boy
and I know we
are never too young
to fall in love.

Look at her old soul;
she has already seen
too much.

She carries the sins
of her mother.
She will do better
than I.

~~~~

Three: Scorpius Exits

Some things are
unforgivable;
I do anyway.

I'll find peace
when Scorpius
exits

Wing my way into
some higher,
stronger self
that is always
overinflated,

indulgent
in small
pieces

I will sleep
soon enough
and how soon
is enough?

Some things are
unforgettable;
I do, anyway.

I'll find grace
when Scorpius
exits.

Ring this rusted
diamond; shape
it into humility,

linger in the
lifeblood
hope dies

I will wake
soon enough
and how soon
is enough?

~~~~~~

And Sleep Will Come

Someone loves me,
I see it in the fire
feel it in the water.

Cleansed in healing words;
they linger as heart notes
when voice falls silent.

There are colours that come
in a life, know where to place
neatly like a fresh package of Crayola's®.

I want to run through an open
meadow where flowers bloom
and passion plays in innocence.

Write silly love songs in the sand
hang glide in the waves that rise
bring salt to lips that are blushed.

~~~~~~

Triple Scoop Sunset

I. Water Like Glass

Children climb this sand dune
in front of the wall where I land.
There is pink underlining
the grey~blue clouds that
hover; hold promise of rain.

Melanie says the clouds
look like the edges of burnt paper
and how clear we can see Coronado
all in one breath.

The surfers play sermon
in the chill of November;
they inhale the darkened water.

I wonder how this wall will hold
up through December.

II. Two Strokes Of A Heart

I missed the glory of the sunset
by two strokes of a heart.
Clouds reign towering Heaven;
full of want, a need to tear.
The pink house sits still
with only an upstairs light on.
There are people living in my dream,
I doubt they are as happy.

There's a crowd scattering,
waves crash in my ears;
sound so intricate.
I find myself here
and wonder
why I don't come more.

The wooden doors close hard
on the shops lining the walk
to the pier.
Water turns black.

III. Still Photographs

I capture word moments
like still photographs.
I see a light far on the water;
lighthouse or boat.
It beckons me to come;
swim the distance.
I'm in training.
There's a hazy white arch
reaching over the heaviest
of grey just above, to my right.
A matter of time to sink or swim.

~~~~~

After The Storm

One:
Ten days later,
I am so very drained
void of emotion
after the storm.

I drink green tea,
with Mandarin orange
and honey jasmine.

Soothing, like the birds
that gather on the shoreline,
the water looks like glass
in the cold light.

I turn south to see
big white tides break.
They are me.

Two:
The day glides away;
I am not swayed.
I should need
a friend to talk to;
someone who can listen.
There is not one.
I put myself in the middle.

The waves crash soft,
then hard; echo.

Three:
I march on, feel my way.
The lifeguard drives by,
there is nothing to guard.

Four:
I've always had angels
in the water.
They don't speak to me.

We're all searching
for everlasting
and the most we can hope for
is clarity; defining moments
that carry us into the
next leg of the journey.

I grow weary on broken
paths and wonder if I ever
make it to the top
of the mountain.

There is no flash forward
and this isn't a competition.

It is the air we breathe,
toxins we release,
ghosts we bury
and final waves.

Linger in spirit,
cling to the sides
edging upward.

Five:
These trees are sturdy,
firmly planted in sand.
They stand tall and proud
letting the wind breeze through.

These are the places
I will remember all my life

Six:
The good water greets
white birds waiting
sustenance.

~~~~~~

In Between Lines Of Oil And Blood

I see the swirling dark
in the starry night,
I've always seen what
lies in between lines
of oil and blood.
I have never known
the full capacity of
any realm I could call
my own.

I have walked through
fires raging storm
only to land heartily
on both feet, standing
with no residual scars.

I swam with sharks
only to be
gently taken in
on the back of
a dolphin.

I feel the curling mark
in the heat of a heart,
I've always felt what
lies we never admit
in
moments of oil and blood.
I have never felt
the full capacity of
any realm I could call
my own.

~~~~~~~

I Don't Know A Thing

1:47 in the morning

waiting as if
some majestic
hue is coming

to shield,

black winter
rivet
holes
through
steel armor

binding blind

I can't keep up
with the pills
or the Joneses
the wavering
ground
underfoot

carries the weak
to knees of strength

I know there is a balance
a tender striking
key;
it hides in grace
and humility

This ivory
I strike with fingers
that have bled
a note too many,
tarried a song
too far

"Not a question"
indeed,
those words
become crystalline

clarity driven

Succumb
silent sun

Alter landscape
of water
make shapes
out of sadness

Weave a wing
away in a mangled manger

time draws us in
close
circle like ravens
until the needle
comes undone

comes into
black spring

December
wilts
by the wall

where I thought
forever held strong

untie unity

~~~~~~~

Holiday Markers

It's coming again,
five years passed
the day
the flesh flew
airborne to land
on back beds
before asphalt.

The prayer,
self-projection,
exhausting
evening of saving
skeletons and blood
only to watch the slow
suffering, daily seizures
end a life.

A breath too soon
drawn upon old
souls, vacuously
take wandering
gypsy soul, brother.

Sins of the sister,
always a balanced
mirror to reflect
back
to me, a sense
of acceptance
among the family,
a place.

Unspoken valence
between genes,
sharing, not a prayer
whispered quietly
in the hushes of
blood, brain, and mortar.

Mayan Moon
rocked to slumber
final curtain calls
rising sun
over ocean
where the hammock
folded neatly into
one.

{for my brother, Jimmy
1949-1998}

~~~~~~

Away From Cold Serpent

The archer knows
moves gently into;
away from cold serpent.
We're heading past
the age of strumming
into finality, fatalistic,
nihilistic desire

I feel the currents
turn, the tide is
nearer the edge
people cry en masse
waves crinkle
under the weight
of angels

It's coming from the
deep, the mysterious
fate we all encounter
one day or another.

Karma, Dharma
and all things
in between.

One quick slash
a wrist snaps;
time elapses
as we know it,
fades the id.

Holding on,
holding out
holding in
we wait on
timelines
divide the spirit
in three.

The balance comes
at last, with liberty
to take ghosts and wrap
them in one vast temple.

It's a day of thinking,
sinking, reflecting,
slice it up, baby.

~~~~~~~~

Wait Light

There is an incredible spray of stars
out my window where waves
crash loud and hard
in the night.

Wait light,
don't leave me here
alone

Life is primed
miracles abound
as we walk
oaths we take;
we can't possibly
honor all that
is here,
sacred ground
beneath leaves

hang apples
on trees made of
cinnamon and light.

Holiday scents
sweep over a childhood
memory; I was growing
nephrite in an empty room.
No one looked deep enough
to touch the fire that has always
raged, never to be.

Wait light,
I am not ready
to catch this ride,
dreams are real.

~~~~~~

Fallen Silence

It's as though
someone muted
the sound around me,
fallen silence in sinking heart.

Bed calls quietly,
soothe me into
colored dreams
lift me to Heaven;
let me see this path
laid out.

My eyes fall fast
into an arena where
time stands
and oceans melt
weight in the flash of a blink.

~~~~~~

Pushing Envelopes

We wanted to push
the envelope of poetry.
Mind~fucking was never
better here in the deep black.
You needed the challenging
range of emotional depth
I bring.

{the endless unknown
stirring of night}

And what will we reap
as seeds scatter;
far corners of ocean~sounds
cry for more.

Swim baby swim,
breathe deep
keep breathing
fire into water
tame flames
trite words
carried over
a threshold
you never knew
existed so deep
within the ever
changing waves.

Watch me turn
to ice, solid
as I whisk
through
a world
of words
and sorrow.

~~~~~~

Monday Blu

I. Cafe Mourning

I do mourning so well
in cafe latte
I didn't bring the phone
downstairs
this morning,
not expecting any calls

The children read,
I write;
We'll play at noon

I go braless most days now,
not bothering to change
sleep clothes

11:45 already

We're reading the cards

they fight

{dull throb pain}
{head vase scatter}
{roses ash black}
{onyx sapphire}
{Sappho Nin}
{vascular}

Splatter all there is
with no time
to focus on one
single thing

wonder if I'm ready
to dive into last night's
dreams

II. Afternoon Quiet

The phone rings
short, broken tones
like a call that can't be
completed

I took 13 pills the other day,
nothing works;
wash me in Novocain

this sick headache
knows no release

III. Early Eve

Nothing is set in stone
there are no good~byes,
except in death.

Voices haunt;
I am stronger, still
this migraine maims

Redefine lines,
places and catalog
the rest; save for other
wounds to bleed on white

Inspiration spills
from bruised abyss
and all I leave is
pain

Wrapped in caffeine
and smoke, there is
no sun to set this day
the grey chills
down to the bone

IV. Night Falls

Who are you today?

Make the night coffee
and make it sweet
to take with sleep

Light a candle
use with caution
and colour therapy

Walk empty midnight
beach, let waves
crash in ears that
ring; cold stone, cold
emotion to be filtered
and used on rainy days

There is no more
than a void here
to capture attention;
drive away demons
that tear in two

~free the demons
from the dungeon
bleed the veins dry~

A zombie crawls
my skin
I sink in myself;
drown in dreams

when I never had the
right to take more
than is allowed

I always take more
need more
want more

Shatter diamonds;
personal poetry, for one

V. Midnight Toss

Sip the syrup
let the elixir
do its trick,
wonder of visions
take me deep

hyperactive brain
let emotion speak
through song
and verse that
break on water
warm fingers over
fiery words
that slip
over ice
un~meltable
device

~~~~~~

Picnic

One:
We throw bread
and cracker crumbs
to the birds who surround
just right of the pink house.

They prattle, beg for more.
We share our picnic,
we talk, they listen,
talk back;
hover above
fly in and out.
The gulls stay
at shore.
We get pigeons
and baby pelicans;
snowbirds at our feet.

We watch ten foot
waves form, break;
majestic view as
the tide comes in.

We are sheltered
atop this mound
of sand piled high
above where we climb.

Two:
Rising from the cellar,
the bright of day
won't let me linger
in the dark.

Bittersweet words
ease into acceptance
of this and all things
right in the world.

I think I know now
what was reaped;
what is.

I walk home
elated; almost high
with the sun on
my back.
I don't know
where this feeling
is born.

Three:

return
to remind me

fragile

in layers
that scream
for comfort,
receive
gift of love
and goddess
dreams
of gold and white,
stand against
the wall that protects
sight in subterranean sable.

~~~~~~

Falling Bed

This is the falling bed
its sheets are jade
and burgundy;
a fine accent
for emotions

that waver
as waves crash;
some nights
loud and hard
then soft and subtle.

I sleep to dream
of days that turn into Heaven
through an open meadow
with flowers and misty green grass.

~~~~~~~

A Place That Hides

There is a place that hides
where we hunger;
need
seek fulfillment;
it isn't God.

A place we seek

ultimate
sublime

Is it insanity?

Lost stance
in Holy Water,
thirst for
Knowledge.

Strike a balance

Waning, waxing
and bleaching
pale illusions
of monogamy;
shake the gold
dust from eyes
that slumber
in dark ages
of Biblical
implications
as dreams
carry forward.

Emote the world
in the palm of one
hand, balance
value in the other.

I am locating
a vast expanse;
what is relative
to my own spirit,
to free the path

leave only scattered
crumbs for those
who hear
to follow.

I like to push ideas

You ask,
with good reason;
a foundation
on which to stand,
is this mere lust
or a true extension
of love; I feel.

Hot sweat
cold fever
passion flair;
honest attempt

Uncover truth

bleed with demons
set angels in flames

Find beauty

Intimacy

Come, count the stars
as we walk this way,
closer to the heart.

I can't stand so close
to remain unaffected
for long; deception

inside track takes
the very dark.

Save your soul

Wing from trees
haunt your own
dreams within
standing out
watching like a
movie being played
expressly for you.

Reap from fallowed fields
with hands gathered.

One falling season

Hold close what
is bright and pure,
final etchings in
a mind, take gentle
strides here.

Smoke a valiant
pipe, it's a slow
world, give them time;
a race that is never
complete.

Unfurl this mass
predict a happier
Eden; home.

Why must it all
be a struggle, finding
worth a noble gesture?

Wander astray,
matter in hands
that ice with
shivers of age,

There is a place
that hides,

I know I am here
somewhere.
~~~~~~~
consume

part one

feel the tears;
let them consume
the chaos of recent
days in hormonal hell;
migraine madness
sweeps the moon,
winning hands down.
there was never
a prayer of coming
out of this alive.

part two

there are little things
that consume our time,
thoughts, take us out
into the Styx,
leave us for dead.

part three

I may as well be
consumed;
better than obsession
I don't know if I ever
get there
what I will do
without the dream

part four

and we are all
consumables;
not consumers
as we are taken
in, viewed from
afar as something
to devour.

~~~~~~

Seven Matches

Light this cigarette
in the sand;
grey like the sky

dark water

chain smoke

Our beach
belongs to no one,

I only came
to write
with a pink backdrop

sip slowly

Ocean ahead
full steam on

it's cold
my bones feel
every breeze
scented with salt

I walk without

~~~~~~~

Medicate

Medicate me
delicate delusion

Dripping flesh
apparition
of Priestess

Enter Dialogue:

Golden eyes
riddles of ribbon

Sheets of forest
trees out of view

Cranberry wishes

Little arrows
in my head

Steely lines
in the air

Slap me silly
into a blizzard of bliss

Bless this blood
Guardian of Idiocy

Fields of Strawberry Lace

Neon Exit:

reach reach

~~~~~~

Phantom Dreams

Dreamscaped:
In broad daylight,
I come to see
maybe there is nothing
significant
in these flashes;
fleeting fragments.

Put aside images
of the day
into the night;

past dreams
surface~visit.

Before sleep:
Moses and Jesus
come out of stone
buildings
holding, shaking staff
at a people.
I could not see left.

The masses
of today
oppose.

Lapse:
Put up reflective tape.
Write in big red lipstick letters:
"Not tonight; I just can't."

Chimera:
A boulevard lined
with palm trees
and street lights
in the middle median,
through fog.

Look to the right;
see mountains.
Look to the left;
see headlights.
Wait to pull out.
Car never comes
to pass.
I can't force
my eyes to look left again.

Prerogative:
And then I feel the shake
beneath my feet.
It trembles, rumbles through
my entire body.

Intricate network
of balance
trip~toe wiring
that stays
in a world of
mesh, lace, and illusion.

Time escapades before
Man was allowed to walk
with eloquence and fear.
A challenge to master a King.

Respite:
I have a strange
comfortable calm
as I drift into dreams
of the night.

~~~~~~

Shadow In Your Breath

Let me walk before you.
Shadow in your breath,
lean into this wave to ride;
home is just a wish away.

Take this with you to sleep
mirror of your soul,
clean as morning's air,
pure as driven snow.

~~~~~~

Inward Drawn

This quiet night;
inward drawn.
A master engineer's plan.
The dust is piled high,
one month out;
it never ends
like laundry
the bills;
the search
for perfect moments.
They creep up
from behind when you aren't
looking. They are born
out of the easiest, most earnest
unrehearsed events.

Watch my smile
practice this gesture;
the way arms sway.
Carry this cross
lay it down in the ash.
Watch it rise
as the sun fades
into the mountain--
the sea waits to catch
its fall.

Chocolate mint candy cane
wishes to wash away
the cares of the world.
Color this in
with hyacinth hues.
One single blade of grass
can cut deeper, sharper
than a missive of swords.

~~~~~~

Indifferently Coloured

The lazy stretch of limbs
yawn and frown;
drug hangover.

And what matters?

Inspiration lies;
holds truth
as if one were holier
than another.

Is there one true
defining moment
in the art of literature?
Was Henry Miller
right about
music, politics, or Anais?

Who can close their
minds to all that has
been historically?

There are small traces
left to learn from, to grow.
Seven years of prosperity
taken with poverty and hunger.
It's a pattern to remember;
embrace the ghosts who have
passed and keep true

ideals and reality
in harmony

~~~~~~

Adoring

I need to sit in the sun,
let it wash over me.
The green outdoors
reflect its goodness.
Pure scent of dirt
when the first rain hits
in between.

I don't need a dream
machine to fire the line.

And please remember
to keep all thoughts
in one whole piece.
No broken valor,
pale significance of separation
of time and emotion.
It all balances in the end.

The river flows
into melted candles.
Light the fire,
close your eyes
say a prayer.
You don't have to
steal a thing.

~~~~~~

No Words To Filter

What weighs so heavy here
keeping me while eyes close;
no words to filter the year,
the silent dance.

Interior design
creates waves
and passion
plays from a past;
distant cry.

People keep passing
before my eyes,
in the streets,
in life.
End life.

~~~~~~

Chains

Chain smoke with coffee
you can't stop
the flow
like lava
once erupted.
How boorish
it all seems -
these fading days
find me closer to nothing.
sigh - exhale -
waste breath.
I can't make a feeling
come when it
wants for nothing.
Erase a life,
leave no trace.
Follow this shadow
line into the back
alley of Hell.
Secret passage
while I stay
dreaming life
in Purgatory.
Wait on line
for the Gate to reopen.
Emerge eagle, rise and shine;
the world is your stage.
Exit left.

~~~~~~

October

November

December

2001

I drive

rote control

mute patrol

reaction fraction

*)

******

Fragile As Ice

My heart could break
fragile as ice
I feel the greenery
rise with water
drips to sweep
over this
this
this
unnamable this.

******

After the Wars

Her face was drawn
battles take their toll
fling survivors to scarce lands

Fiercely determined
to save her own
she lay in the grave earth
in hushed tones
tapped her way out
to a freedom
she had only dreamed

Fallen soldiers
she tripped over
blood and ash
to light

They couldn't see
eye to eye
so someone took
an eye for an eye

and now
we all pay

****

Turns On Its Ass

I'm sick of talk radio
so I turn on some
familiar Sarah
songs
*"..in terms of endearment.."
but I know that isn't
the real title
it's what I call it, anyway.
I'm sick up to here
of hearing about
the war, the bombs,
the hungry children
in Afghanistan
and how they'll starve
this winter,
a harsh winter ahead.
"Send one dollar in to
the White House
to help feed the children
in war-torn Afghanistan."
Isn't there some sort
of sick, twisted irony
in this request?
Make the children of America
feel good, a little less guilty
to feed the children
we don't kill.
Collateral damage.
Feed them patriotism
on a yardstick
so they'll grow up
to defend truth
honor
liberty
and justice for all.
Whose truths?

I don't want to be a proud mother
of a dead soldier.
I'm sick of hearing
the propaganda on all sides
of every coin.
I read and read and read
and I know I don't know
what to believe.
Dr. Laura
with her
"now go do the right thing."
as if she is the only person
alive, who knows what
the right thing is
and must honestly believe
none of us are doing it.
I am reclusive
and have been out of touch
but where was I when
this new breed took over,
to command our world?
I talk, I write, I listen,
I hear whispers
and shouts
in the streets,
in my sleep
in the world
at large
as it turns on its
ass.
I'm sick of it all
I need to breathe
and dream
in full stereo-boom
surround-sound,
vivid technicolor vision
like I am accustomed to.
I know my needs
outweigh reality
and fall
out of sync

with the norm.
So what?!
I live, I breathe
I walk and seethe
this straight line
of right
and truth.
I awe at the ignorance
seen in such levels
of disgrace.
Where the hell
was I when this new breed
was born?
And now I am told
the F.B.I. has files on
each and every one of us.
I am naive.
I slip
but
survive.
And I wonder
how many erroneous
"facts"
are stored
in the files -
yours,
mine...

and all the while
the world turns
on its ass.

******

Utopia?

Who wants utopia
when we have war
and hell
prospering
our future?

******

No Great Mountain

You say
I'm fatalistic
because I have no great
mountain to scale
before I die

Am I not the optimist
among friends
who says the Tribulation
is at hand
while the hand
of God guides me
to believe

I, innocent fool
to think there are
parties who
wish us to think
the end is here
by manipulation
of prophecies
and Revelations

I, like Patty
look forward
to the rest of my life
however
long or short
that may be

****

Song

I.
The storm passed
it came without warning
left plenty of damage

We spend the next day
sewing clipped wings
and listen to ravens

gather and squawk
they drown out voice
and unwanted noises

I bide time
weigh energy
collect raindrops

Let the sun reign
down my back
regenerate frayed nerves

II.
Jagged stupor
eruption of tears
one Christmas song

brings me back
to a night in November
as the wine spilled

easy over celery and onion
a priest to be called
and everything shattered

One phone call
spiraled out
spun down

Condensed sobriety
project self
to save a life

the power of prayer
kept from death
fall into cold concrete

hard sleep
Thanksgiving morning
found forgiving Father

Always a holiday
dread the season
no one to blame

******

Familiarity

Maybe

my heart
would still race
if I were to come
eye to eye

count two

And

I wonder
if it is familiarity
that breeds
ease
of heartbeat

Or

If there is genuine
emotion
to count
among the tides
while catching breath

That

I shouldn't have lost
just because
a short walk
to stare
into glass
and meditate
write
heal
something deeper

that cannot
be touched
nor traced
to any of this

took

time to see

******

The Fear Of Change

And when I bleed
I bleed loud and clear
putonashow
for all to see
and smell
the fear
of change

Because I know
nothing will come
of it
maskthetide
for none to know
and deny
the tear
of derange

I heard somewhere
about a black hole
leading to a white hole
and the entrance
to heaven
is just a breath
awayinamanger
we all sing
Christmas
hymns
this time of year
rearranged

displaced by winter
that never comes

we allliveonforever
in everlasting
peace
harmony
that
isn't reserved
for the few
in a distant lair
on a binge

is it 144,000
last count?

.

.

******

Should I

Should I take it
all back,
should I take it?
Should I step back
and
look more closely
into the words
I drop
without
thought?

I should think things
through
more closely
before I spout

Not that it matters

I feel like
Sexton
in her
last years

lately

close proximity
but I don't
commit
acts
of

insanity
with such
ease
and
elegance

There are
no Paris Review
or New Yorker
credits
to add
to the dismal
list

of who cares
anyway
where you've been

and

where you haven't

I've turned from Anais
complex
to Anne
bruised
black
grey
and blu

in swells
of no apparent
reason
or forewarning

just comes

lights

stays

stirs

claws

90

The children
go to the beach
to play
soccer

give me peace
to mark
before
the break
has its way

I wind back
into comfort

because

it's
all so very
important

******

Nearing Birth

I want to know
how the moon moves

storms

I'm letting them
have the war
without me

"What war?"
my friend says back to me
when I ask
how it is playing
across the Atlantic

I weighed
all the evidence
and stories;
decided to let it be

^sanp snap^

on my own

without trial
fire fury

there is a fire
still

The dreams
come and go
phases
phraseology
to match some
politico drama

I don't indulge

I used to be
a prime candidate
for the Bill Maher Hour

I don't watch tv
I can't participate

The wrist flecks
twists in false
chain
of {common} command

Today was the day
I held back

a veil
and let life be*

93

******

Half The Battle

As I lay me down:
Forget everything
you ever knew
about love

I won half the battle
but I don't know
what the other half is

You're about to see
a whole new way
to live

It's all about knowledge
trust camouflage
intimate cries

Still waiting for news
about the war
I won't be a part

I can't make a connection
tie anything to anything
but forever is forever

apologist;
I rather like that word
its meaning and connotation

as if the world hinges
on one blind word
that only reminds me

to sleep:
I dreamt of holding a baby
a blind woman
a deaf woman

I told the other lady
she had to help them
because she was stronger

{images}:
A packed garage
with the little red car
on its side

One chocolate pie
doesn't go far
when serving a crowd

those who aren't allowed
to consume riches
and the others devoured

what was left
small measure
to look at

I pray the Lord:
Sunday morning coffee
hungover from love
and thigh-high cramps

my soul to keep:
Sort spindle and manipulate
tortures of the mind
split wide open

if I should die:
in space
in minds
my coffee's cold

{before I wake,
I pray the Lord
my soul to take}

******

Stealing

Someone's stealing my act
I've not seen
hide nor heir

slow morning fall
heavy layer
of drift

It's dead here
with only a few
to show

keep your head
above balance
let the scream out

I am going to read
from the past
try to see why they do

This is looking epic
in proportion to actuality
eventually we cling to ghosts

Simple equation:
I'm happy just to be
nothing more, nothing less

See? it's all what we make
every dreamer's sin
every thinker's id

How can any one thing
alter what has been laid
in veins by the time before time?

Someone's holding Mass
smoke another incense stick
smolder the candle in a shroud

Castrate the mind
hold court in secret chamber
where 1984 reigns

They can't break me
they can't take my pleasure
in sick mind control

Flip the dials
spin the wave
I am only here for brevity's sake

I think
I should go back
and add the dots and cross the tease

Slow dancer
hold me close
as we sink into never

******

I Feel The Moon Stir

I feel the moon
stir
and
I see
it makes no sense
to you
that isn't
my bad
my fault
lines only
the narrow
passageways
through
the center
I can't sleep
I may as well
be here;
toil in the tether

Slow day
wait for answer
deadline met

exultation

euphoric
he said
an emotion
I don't catalog
well

I'll find breaks
to drive you
mad
as we are

in this time
in any time

what is the difference
the defining moment
that kneads
your memoir
any neater
or better
than any other?

Ah, it isn't as it seems
now is it?

******

Presents Presence

I was always falling
in love with someone
who looked better
than what the present
presented
and
in this presence
of preset personas
I find small comfort
and a laugh
I allow only to myself

Abstract apparition
as if I could spell
or cast them to a wall
that runs parallel
to the ocean of my heart

There is only a beat
away to tomorrow
and a bat of a lash
to yesterday
to claim;
reclaim
the missing pieces
while the bridge stands
as ever
as the dream foretold
in a tiny town
somewhere around
Savannah

Someone's backyard
it wasn't the same
as the one we looked
at today

through the fog
and dim, hazy shade
of maize

The trees
effervescent

I never made it back
to the east coast,
the south
goes on without me
and
I am sure there are too
many changes I couldn't
face

even in the day

ghosts come out
to play
with no fear
or repercussion

acts of kindness
go unnoticed
by the masses

The presence
of presents
and slow memory
makes
a day sad
with bursts
of joy
that come to the surface

quiet nudge
surreal thought

walk away

I'm not selling
a thing

******

Maybe It Is The Moon

Maybe it is the moon
slicing up the phases
of the day
tearing at
ninety to nothing
inside where
it all lies
buried

Pass the key
this way

Climb the vine
head up through
the maze

Diamonds shatter

Maybe I am insane
after all

a common thread
I pull almost daily

what is this
tug

******

Random Fallout

It's nothing more
than random fallout
springs from sapphire's
mist and diamond's rust

And I wonder
about the icecaps
on the moon's surface
the tides here at home
into the Pacific
where I spill

the breakage
does little
to repair
loss

Turn now
one walk
from eternity
frames

Flames surrender

I don't have the stomach
for this

It's vacant
empty
of light

a comfort
to be held

******

Arch

I arch with archaic words
to stretch across the sky
reach in to take your very
eyes into mine

titles and names
to shed the skin
that wraps tight
under flesh

Dharma always seems
to work well
wherever we can etch it in

I know I am followed
when they think
I am not looking
I see it all

take stares
with the glory

it's all part
of intricate
pattern

Patriotic hero
fallen pope
of some sordid
century

They laugh

insidious sin

ignorance

106

has a sense
all it's own

or

they just run
in fear
and prejudice
that blinds
the open market
on any given
bright day

while the clouds
hover
the fog rolls

I feign
sweet denial
of betrayal
leave a trail
of crumbs
for the pagans
to lap up

******

Hook Line and Sinker

She slithered back
in her chair
the one by the ocean
on the rooftop deck;
easy in her glance,
a nod from here
to the end of the World.

She knew he knew
by the look in his eyes
that told everything
he couldn't bear;
everything he couldn't bring
through his lips.
The words formed
only in his head
as The Tower
toppled
on cue.

Impending doom
luminous in its view;
she took the holy cloth
from his head
draped the blood-soaked
chambray
to make a crown
to place on the infant's
tomb.

In another city
a Hermit lights the way;
carries gifts
with the orphan
to bestow
upon the Queen's

palm.

And in the end
The Hierophant
preached
loud and clear
for all pagans
to take
home across the water;
their swords
laid to rest.

The next day
The Moon sunk
deep and low
over the river
as The Sun
shone
in another direction
toward
ultimate declarations
of peace.

The Star
could only draw
more water
to spread
with invariant
parts
to the sum of
The Fool.

In the beginning
there was.

******

Prick

Prick the skin
with gentle
quiver

I drink cold
coffee because
the walk down
is too much

Take the words
down slow
with precise
circumspection

a light lingers
where you left

energy displaced
like a ghost's
walkthrough
brilliance

and flowers
scent the stratosphere

It's in the senses
we grow
tend to
as though
it is the cure-all

and

maybe

it is

You stroke
wildly
at the canvas

open air
circus

just to see
the audience
light
with awe
and aware
nuance

you like to place
under your pillow

a vision
to take
dreamland
to new heights

Could this feel
any better
at this moment
this air
flowing
through
with no enterprise
no emancipation
sudden vitality
in veins
out of water's ilk

******

Another Trojan Horse

I stumble
over words
today
like
another Trojan
Horse
stampede
through
this house
inside
where tremors
reside
snugly
in womb

This new
day of nostalgia
leaves me
blank
empty
to remember
something
that was only
what I wanted

it was my dream;

you had your own

******

Breathe Baby Breathe

Part One:
There are always
events that stir
the dosage of crisis
and trial you need.

Set the parameters,
limit the entourage
that encircles you;
takes all
the blood you can muster.

Step back,
breathe baby breathe.

All I can do is listen.
A vacant whisper
I send a safe house
to fall when the madness
takes your last ounce.

A soft meadow
is a dream
with bright
balloons
that send
missives
of platonic love.

Part Two:
And we've shifted
into a place
I pretend to be content.

It stirs no matter.

I see a balance
on the horizon
but it is out of reach.

And some words
cut like diamonds;
leaves rust
to scour
away tears
and fibers
that remain.

******

Extremes

I need extremes
something
to make this
blood flow
free
of resin
left
by too many
wannabe lovers
who could never
test the water
out of season

the rivers
flowed

they withered
before
their eyes could adjust

I'm still waiting
for that one
who can match
my spirit
my extreme
my stride
to take
a stand
where
life is shrouded
beyond time

and

the water
crests
over
a body
waiting
for someone

to take my breath
with words
that melt,

where no one sees

I need extremes

******

Hunt
/
Gather

Blunt   cut
pale   glance
seeks   same
soul   folk
soft   speak
red   blue
simple food
brain   auction
fast   rise
beat   slow

storm   rage
deny   inflection
tone   ray
deaf   palm
rain   gentle
mice   make
man   made
river   flow
***   ***

******

Over The Ledge

I just needed
some water
to carry me
through

over the ledge

Kiss my mustard lips
and put me to bed

midnight snack
at nine p.m.
because
the day has
been too long
without sleep

Line your cards
let me choose
the path

I waver
long enough
to think it through

and

I know I tend
to cling too long,

save me some grace

I take tea
with pain
and aspirin
for fear

Loss
in coveted shades

for comfort

at this stage
it's all so
over the edge

at any rate
what's in a conviction

******

Sewn In Blood

A lovefest presides
over heavy night breath
that thinks it can contrive
an alternative
to what is sewn in blood

It's raw
like nerves
that are fried
from overdose
of life

There lies
a sweet silence
to all of this

a quiet knowing
of times past

and

what lies
in future
hands
that do not know
the right
path

yet

I hate to see you
wallow in the mud
with the trash
that comes
takes spirit
to make their own

soar

in reflective light

that's all there is
in some

a shadow
of brilliance

overpowers
psyche

gleams
a brighter
shallow moment

fleeting

******

Subterranean

One:
A darker layer
emerges

lacerated
paragon

I've known a different
parable all these years

it's like being hit
with a 2x4

Sudden insight
of so many things
that have come
and fallen
at my feet

through birthright

Two:
Maybe
it was her gift

she passed

without
much supposition

and

I always thought
it had something
to do with blood sugar

Three:
Funny,
it would appear;

descend on a night like this

when all is right
with the world

two days
now
in happy
snappy
joy

SMACK

just like
the other shoe

Four:
I've yet to see
veracity

come forth

face
to
face

with the accuser

the teller
of tales

swathed in secure
silent location
where imagination
can run

barter
dreams
with
phantasm

Five:
It all makes
perfect sense

when you unveil
a layer at a time

expose overlay
of time
trial
and
a truth
you knew
somewhere
in the subsurface

******

You Do

It's a long path
ahead
and
I don't see where
it meets
in any middle

You're doing church
duty
while I watch
the waves

There's a balance
here
and I think
about it all the time

Home now
to research
family trees
and genetics
that likely play
a part
in who
I am

New inspiration
scrapes
gentle here

a new vein
to splice

Maybe I am lulled
into a false sense
of security

with time
comes
familiarity
and ease
of emotion

that lies
in the flesh

the wounds
on open display

I am only reaching
understanding
of truth
as it really
happened
and
not some delusionary
style of story

Fiction breeds
among the vines;
take your breath
and walk
the forest

find the light
within the foliage
and flowers
that bloom
at night

I'll deal the cards
and tell you
a tale
of mystery
and
enchantment
that will raise

the hair
on your neck

If there is a connection
to be made
a voice
to be heard
it will not go
unnoticed

******

Hanging Ghosts

PreRamble:
Ghosts only hang
as long as you let them

Prologue:
In this time
of suicidal
revenge
I find

I am hypersensitive

Dialogue:
I thought
as I drove
about
multifarious
attachment

how
it always
finds me

in dithers
and torn

from one post
to the next

Comparative weighing
of the senses
and the balance
that does not
fit

and

Why should I come
in layers
dual
doses

Does it make
one less
than the other?

Soliloquy:

a layman's
terminology
pivots

on end
on line

we wait
like good
ant soldiers
who want
for nothing
more
than to serve

the enemy

Epilogue:
The bell rings;
A sprite is stimulated
who lives
nearby

Post Script:
Simplicity;
ample souvenirs
to keep
when winter dies

It's always
another Rome
to build

overnight

******

Spill Me

Spill me
from the wood
cast in steel
ground
as flawless grace
walks
on time

I want to embrace
an era
when I knew
by rote
how to carry;
measure moments
and
life was

******

Dance

It's the dance
slow
steady
against my cheek
against time

a comfort
morning

I am going to sit
in bed and read
some of the old greats
while sipping
memories

It is the dance
that keeps us
tied in knots

one step forward
three back
the pages
of life

I am going to sit
by the ocean
and listen
to the great waves
that roar,
let the scent
of the spray
cover
my face

someday
the hermit
will unveil
all the secrets
we need

and we'll dance
in white
motionless
perfection

******

Decanter and Dominoes

My decanter is
cobalt blue,
thin and slick
like the emotions
that slip
through.
Its contents swish
and swirl
against a Southern
backdrop.

Anointed with holy water
it levitates high over
the moon
purifies the ocean
that passes
through lips
painted a soft
shade of mauve.

Cherry mahogany inside
where tar
lingers;
creates new hope
out of desperate dreams.

It is only an apparition
from another realm
where we walk
at night
on toes under
cedar and ash
in the illuminated
spirits that rise
from deep wells
not meant

for public consumption.

We adorn
our souls
with mighty
swords
that breathe
us back
to this midnight eve.

Tears are
for cleansing
consecrated omnipotent
walls that collect rain
to make undiminished
sleep authentic.

Toxin-free
held rein
to speak
to see
beyond the stars
where legends
sketch in perfect harmony
with immaculate
expression.

******

Next To The Rich Wood Panels

I am about to sleep
with shadows
as they play
on the lace
next to the rich
wood panels

I am about to dream
with shallow
visions as they dance
under the lids
of blackened circles
that covet the soul

I am about
so much more
than you
credit the bows with
as the words
take hold
and triggers
are on the fingertips
of paradise

******

It Is The More

I begin

It is the more
that cannot
be explained
that I want
to know of

but

I don't want
to write reactionary
journalistic
drivel

I am driven
beyond
what stars
measure
with any earthly
possession

This mansion
has cracked
walls that seep
the debris
when it is dark
and unfilled

Laughter roars
through halls
that are dimly lit
in honor of
six-year anniversary

I stood by the water's edge
and watched
the ocean rip
tides that kissed
the top of the pier

and
wondered in awe
at the gifts
that have been
given

and those
taken without
a polite hello

I worshipped
at the storm's
front door;
the foot
of the shore
and said a silent
prayer
for my brother
who died

******

As They Come

It feels
so good
to lie
in the sand
watch the enormous
waves as they come

I turn
to take sight
of my pink house

a middle-aged
man comes out
lights a cigarette
and walks around
the enclosed patio
where the fountain
is still

It is my house
why is he there?

I watch his movement
and can see
he doesn't belong

I see a window
raised on the side
of the house
but no face
shows itself

I roll back
to the ocean
feel the roar
in my chest

I read about
the life of
Dylan Thomas
the man
the poet
the person

I think about
writing
but decide
to just inhale
the moments
and scenery

the waterscape
that envelope
every pore
and in between
the marrow

where I can
embrace
his words
that we are
a poet for an hour
a scientist for a week
but an ordinary person
most of the time

He must have been
like the male
High Priestess
who walks the earth
holding secrets
and truth
sacred
alone

******

We're Not In Kansas Anymore

The evening quill
comes gently
through midnight

Ever seeping
searching sin
to cleanse spirit

Morning falls
grace upon lips
sweet as honey

A faded photograph
shows small details
of lost innocence

Child becomes
chilled picture
a framework to paint

Fill in missing links
connect the dots
cross the t's

Too soon to know
dark cellar mystery
unwound in sleep

Dreamscapes to land
in heart where holes
filter the light

Scrubbed with bleach
the sink of soul
a whiter wight

To lend, to hold
faltered species
we grew up without care

Loud voice
shatters thought
in progress

Halted to rest
in red reverie
uneven bricks

Crimson haunted
eyes that speak
a precious sapphire

******

Sapphire's Fire

It's true,
I've been
word~impotent
since Sapphire's
fire swept through

and
I am over
the school girl
crush

it's safe
to come
back
out to play

where we melt
within ocean
walls
and fretter
through
tripped minds
of lace and frill

Jupiter doesn't
crash on cue
it just floats
somewhere
in my memory

I am not lonely
for company
surrounded
with more
than I can handle

but

I never got a handle
on this

******

Not To Be Bothered

It'd be so easy
to turn over
and cave
into fickle demands
of non-prolific
madness.

I need some time
to meditate;
bring ambiance
into symmetry.

It's a private quest
but you're welcome
to watch.

I don't force-feed,
there is no gun
in your head.

Know your audience
annihilate the rest;
a mental exercise.

Junkmen - a dime a dozen
a breather for the failing
invalid.

It's only middle age
that makes you crazy;
it passes with acceptance
and tolerance.

******

Argument

I argued deep
into the night
with God and rage
alternating
with pain
and despair.

Rewards come
in small consequences
that make a life.

The dreams tell me
what I don't want
to know or do
but I will.

Questions,
tests and more tests
of blood, urine
and will.

Flying colours
suspend the day
to halt
and caress the good.

Shower me
with all I can
receive
and I will give
more than I earn.

Desensitized;
the trauma
will come
later

and how long
recovery?

******

37 Years Ago

There I was
being 8
and strong
for her

Comfort for
an old woman
who remembers
every detail
of the day
37 years ago

She cried into
the phone
while I prepared
dinner
for the living

She said she didn't
understand
why she couldn't
get over his death
after all these years

I told her
some things we never
get over;
they just ease with time

It's an old
cliche
that I know
isn't necessarily true
but it gave her
something
to cling to

148

in dark winter

She brings it to
herself
and makes
the pilgrimage
in her mind
every chance
she gets

Sacrament
out of air

It still affects
us all
to a degree

Still,
I am the baby child
who offers kind
reassuring words
on days like these
and comfort foods
for the healing

******

Sip

One:
Last straw
final blow
the wind
doesn't sing
God doesn't
listen
I'm out of prayer
out of knees
to bend
gold
in any manner
that will matter
My ticket's been punched
it runs out at midnight
time to fake a new one
cut a path
to the palace

Two:
Why can't you be happy
even in the center
of the ocean
where drowning
is a familiar comfort?

There is
shame to share
and I'll be damned
if I know
when I grew
this nasty shade
of guilt
I forced it
when indifference
bore me

straight through
the core

Three:
Nothing connects
and dreams
are a vacant memory

******

Neon Church

I am full
of life
but
I singe it

and

pain feels
like a warm
blanket of comfort

evasion of emotion

It's what keeps you
running on full tilt
high-speed overdrive

stop
breathe
feel the words
as they dance;

they're not all bad

******

On The Edge of Eve

I laugh with a mute mouth
show a vacant smile
and deny gently

I wanted to tell her
how many meals
I went without
this last year
so my children
could eat,
or have a lunch
to take to school

I wanted to tell her
of all the nights
we ate peanut butter sandwiches
on crackers
or eggs
or soup made from scraps
in the pantry

and
how hunger feels

I wanted to tell her
how often have I had to choose
between groceries
or things my children
needed, like clothes
or school supplies.

And that he and I
bought nothing
for each other
this year,
for our birthdays,

anniversary
or Christmas

And that just a week ago
we ate sandwiches
made from the dollar store
chopped meats
because I sent Mom
the grocery money
so she could eat

But
I held my tongue
and let the day end
with merry wishes
and stress-free hugs

And tomorrow,
for one day
in the year,
we will eat
a hearty meal
as our gift.

We'll give thanks
that we have each other
and good health
and make happy times
out of the little
we have
in our tiny castle
by the sea.

******

Isn't Safe To Run

It isn't
a punishing act
or a class displacement

it is merely
a lack
of things

I lost along the way
in this torrential
downpour
of emotion
that creaks
the bones
and muscles
deep
under
the layers
where it isn't
safe
to run

There is still
so far, to grow
and room to flex
without words
that cut harshly
tear at the skin
where I don't
want to look

like scratching
the cornea
without warning

it just comes
at you
and the best
you can do
is find refuge
in the rain
while the sun
beats
brow against brew

heavy throttle
up
"don't look down"

surrounds
and you swim
just as the water
covers
your mouth

******

More Than A Moment's Glance

I desperately tried
to find others
to replace
you

over time
it rolls
and you can only
hold your breath
with your thoughts

that smother
and it is only
on grey, nostalgic
days I give it
more than a moment's
glance

I find my middle
best
in this medium
when it finds me
solid and ready
to stand;
deliver
what has been breeding

"This will be an interesting read."
I tell myself
knowing I have been here
before
as I slowly slip
in; recognize
the wallpaper

I suddenly don't care
about hiding
true stories
and identities
that wield
fleshy timbre towers

and
Savannah
never smelled sweeter
or more foreign

******

Of Nothing

Middle-class snobbery
second generation

I bang away
like there is
no midnight
no sleepy words
to covet the flesh

only meaty
memories
when youth
took grace
hid the innocent
naive trace

I tingle
in the numb
night
that comes

there is a hope
that red tinged
slivers
will chip
with ease

fall heavy
under spell
of dreamland
wonder

and
exist within
the walls
of vellum

159

It is the nothing
that kills
faster than smoke
rises out of ash
tarred lungs
still beat
empty heart-paces
just inside
the compound

where the chamber
releases
its star target
on cue

ready at the arms

******

In Tone

Deaf ears somber:
Sometimes
I am mute
the words
just sit there
in my head
the back of my tongue
sits idle
waiting
for them to form
through
pouty lips
that are sealed
from within

I hear;
do I not?
It is like a tape delay
words pass through
like invisible ghosts
walking through
skin
without asking

I hear afterthoughts,
beg to speak
I stop and ask
again what was said
like I departed
this dimension
for dementia
or someplace
safe

******

The Spray

The ocean's mist
sprays my face

the waves
roar close
and fast

an unspoiled
section of the beach
where few come

the water
splashes the rocks
where we sit
writing our
New Year's Resolutions
******

October

November

December

2002

Word

Word interrupt us

before I can snap

them together

like Lego's

*)

******

Armageddon Fever

Twenty minutes
to new skin
new air to cover
politics of the day
Armageddon at our foot-heels
that push hard to forget

it could happen any time now

My throat is no clearer
than before
made worse by smoke
forced through tubes;

can it matter?

Sip tepid water
to soothe tiny
fracture

Light another drag
steal another's time

Find some happy reading
a solace sort of existence
at best; at worst we crack
under stressors of the hour
and call a black kettle for tea
to smooth the edges
so we don't fall under
the stars
and heathen gods

Vagrant Gothic Nirvana

Take that empty needle from your vein
I need you here on planet earth
as long as I remain

Selfish? yeah, that's me
not a virgin thought in sight
a simple stitch to sew your woes
into the dreary night

Please! Don't ask me to make sense
of ludicrous limericks as they leave
all that is pure and sane

Small stop wonder
to glee and gleam
from God's great scheme
of all that we can tame

Surely it is written
in a book larger than us
your time incomplete
upon this gravely turf

I see a gold glint
splinter from your sight
don't look behind
don't look to beggars
and put away that knife

There's no time to dilly dally
the end is close enough
make way for all that comes
into this life-like valley

Full blossom waits to be
garnered as the daisy

you picked when you were lazy
back in the summer days
before the lunacy erupted

You know the way
it's always been
the way we come
to seed

the way you shift from
dawn to dusk
while harbor lights glimmer
upon an ancient river

Come with me now
to see the splendor
awaiting all who venture
with eyes like ours

ever meant to shimmer

******

Catechism and Patriotism

I pledge up patriotism on a platter;
give them God as grace

all the necessary things
to be a good, Catholic American
and wonder in the recess
if this is what I truly want
for them;
a bare minimum of subsistence

Homogenized smiles
spoon-fed thru plastic
cell of energy; list support

Prohibition in secular
wide   open   spaced
Midwest
and
somewhere near North Texas

homespun tales to take
to the grave
turn the dirt once
and walk away

There's a war brewing
I don't want
them anywhere near
lines of fuse-bombs
or enemy camps
where shadows fly
on the half-hour

I'm here for the night
2 by 2 square of heaven
inside wall to wall;

uninhibited silence never fit better

I read with passion
empty words
that fill in to show
rather than tell;
it's the same in life
as poetry
raising eager brilliance
to a higher revelation
where ever is seen
in cited vision
born of gifted sense

Somewhere in the mist
they will find their own
voice and stature
to carry a new generation

I can't listen to nay-sayers
who speak of Armageddon;
not while I have a chasm of breath
left to finish the work

******

To Steal What Never Dies

Sometimes I think
you forget about me
then I remember
we are busy working
the days of our chosen walk;

I'm running out of smoke
and I've long since run
out of gold
to barter any banter.
I might wish to steal
like your time
taken with frozen
blank spots shed
from a lain memory

Pick up another day
disconnect the tone
as if those words
somehow cohesively
made us
more than god
and goddess

We were never meant
to bend like the tree
you left behind
in some Middle America
you can't call home

Home was just a whisper
we invented to comfort
old wounds that never die

******

Leftovers

Leftover emotion seeps
even though I kill it
with prayer;
beg release of pathos

I want to devour
something deep
and rich
that will
exonerate fervor
for that missing space

Can I sit still
long enough
to bring semblance
of civility
into view
without
spectacle
or circumstance?

There was a time
when voice softened
shattered skin;
symmetric
in form
in shape
of two
to become one

This two minute
ground sirloin patty
can't be all there is

I dreamed of a shallow
fire and work
that left me with no equipoise

******

Worst of it All

I have reading to do
stacked sky-high
catch up on what's been missed

in between scraps
and pieces of tangible
wishes blended with
invisible fissure

Inside, where beats
and words fall out of place
interrupt the flow of ideas
and random strings
come; loosen, hasten

A divine right to sanity
a fine line to whisper
on first moons
last moons
and the precious
crescent shape
I lay next to your skin

******

AirStrike

Running ninety to nothing
can't sit still
I am hit
but choose to ignore
blended cries
that sweep the dirt

Cuts catch
where I can barely breathe
faster than the inside
track will take me

I fear
I need something
to calm this stir
this whirl
that whispers
run
run
run
run
like there will be no morning

Adversity comes quick
I know it's there
waiting to strike

in not-so-invisible cover
we are only blinded
by its magnitude
and sweat on the brow

sheer illusion
waits to implode
camaraderie
and

society
as we know it

to split;
we are not so
indivisible
to conquer
virtuous valor.

God lurks

watches
waits
to release His wrath
when we least expect it

or rescue
what is left
of death
and desolation

There's a quiet minority
taking leave of America
and I wanted to be on
that boat
that moves
in sacred circles;
away from war and hate
and violent acts
of disturbance

we are all disturbed;
disrupted
even if we allege
a matrix existence

I feel my heart quicken
my pace slow
suffocation
is imminent
as lungs expand

then collapse.

Lucid images come
in repose; while walking
adrenaline addiction
covets, covert animation

control voice patterns
steady gait
to survive

Noble gestures greet
the enemy eye to eye
it's a subliminal culture
no one talks about
searching front lines
with valiant death~wish

Born under a cold, combative moon
and compulsive inherent attributes
I would wear this suit well

Nihilism at its height
warriors don't come home
unscathed
there has never been
an admirable battle

This isn't sport

******

Nature

The world turns;
changes from day
to night
with increasing violence
of a different nature

lack of respect
for life in heavy doses
is more than I can handle

I break down
inside; keep steady
face front
a shame what we
allow

The antichrist is alive
and well, seeks war
and hate perpetuates
evil in the best of folk

There's a beast
we harbor
I don't know about marks
and signs
all I know is
we live among
some of the worst
of the lot

Is there nowhere
to take cover?
Is there a safe place
to nurture good
and what is right
and just?

Invisible tears
well inside
afraid to release
an ocean's worth
of emotion
ready to erupt

I can't feed
this hunger

******

Gerund Junkie

And the words were falling
faster than I could catch

I wrote them all down
in a fresh opening drawer;
a book of days
that left me
as I shed summer
five years past

Sometimes, when I'm not looking,
the images come crashing
all around me
like snow in Vermont
with the scent of maple
wafting the air

Cold water running
over steamed skin
bottles breaking
sin under a blanket
of pure white

Ghosts take their cue
when I've had more than
the surrogating friend
has allotted

No need
for punctuation
when punching
your way through
the flurry
of seasons

Gender confusing

roles we are playing
in light of every day;
everyman finds his own
battles to forge

and this is just
a splashing
of verbiage
to keep the lineage
warm and dry

******

To Find

Desperate;
too harsh
a cry

disparage;
unknown origin

never to seek
a thing
when things
find me

Deliver me from
sin; ripen rich reward

under a savior moon

I want something
brilliant
and superfluous
to run 'round the sphere
of adorning masses
where the meek adjoin

a stitch in side
weathers
a fine layer
of broken glass

lacerated burns
glow-fire
from somewhere
out of range

I mainline
words

just for the rush;
inebriated aperture

grievous grace
as if there were
an oxymoron to be found
surely it will find
its way into this
artery

******

AngelBreak

My angels break
sound
soft carpet
catches the fall
in ceramic pieces

Accidental violence
erupts from miscommunication
a device this demon
utilizes when the moon
is still; silent

the earth turns
to wave a wand
to create disturbances
among tribal ritual

Cut down reality
back room entry
stealth stealing
moves closer in
to take every bit
of peace
to shatters

My angel breaks
and no one hears
a sound

******

Season With Care

We outgrew the surface of mass
beneath hearts that wore weary
traded tragedy for surreal images
to hang on delicate trees
in the shade of morning

A blush falls over your face
I whisper secrets from archaic
files formed from memory
no need to trudge history
around like a noose
no one can fault
the innocent

Who would jump here
when winter creeps ever
closer? Autumn, a small
deterrent to indifference
a season to smile into
step along the shore
where shells are thrown
like emotion you keep
in check

Guide my hand, my fingers
as they move across the scenery
so smooth a finish inlaid
like marble fresh from Italy
overworked empty jars
to fill with black coffee

Make morning a toasty warm
sensation we all crave
in the season of Christmas
with orange spice cinnamon mix
filtering the air

******

The Sport of Ever
{Sentimental Entreaty}

Final destination
slipped thru vacant
whispers
gossip that left
questions
and
doubt

I'm not supposed to think
about this
but here it is

a date that can't
be erased

so easily
we mute
what was
only a dream
after all

A sinking emotion
haunts skin
chills the marrow

And you're gone
somewhere out of reach
out of sync

Is this really better?

Always needing proof
as if I were from
Missouri

oh! show me that smile
once more
open that crevice
that leads to a chasm

I still don't have the blood
sport for this

Once, we believed
in fate, open gates
and eternal wishes
that bound us in
something deeper
than your leather,
my lace

a chalked cue-stick
smile that melted
heaven right here
in my heart
in your mind
we created
something real
and lasting

like an ocean
and a house
on a hill

or a sapphire
wrapped by one
treasured diamond

Tell me,
is this really better now?

******

Shame on Sham Shaman

Deliver the goods
that prove you
are not a false prophet

Hasn't it been this way
since time began?

This is not a lynch mob
a mere faction who
seek truth
through clear, concise eyes

sieved thru open channels
closed hearts

I profess:
if you were so true
there would be no need
to spew negative jibes
at we, simple sinners
of the soil

Even Jesus broke down
to the apostles
in lucid syntax
parables
to carry forth
the Word

We are past biblical times
and in need of cloudless
bearings
that will indeed take us
to Zion
or exalted nirvana

******

Its Turn

It feels like cancer;
smells like disease -
a scent catalogued
as death took its turn

I sat in an isolated corner
to wait it out

naive innocence
a child inside a child

as if I would know
what cancer feels like
when only vague memories
tell me what I felt
thru his eyes

mortality catches
up with me
new slants come
as day of birth approaches

Needless worry
haunts a tightening gait

I enter
a new phase
and make choices
for another 46 years

******

To Serve

Weights and measures
hold a lie's place
among meek
humble servants

A purpose amid
chaos, a traveler
weary on a path
that never ends

Gold that cannot
be dug or found
in the swells
of God's oceans

Tears that mount
against the tide
toward the heavenly gate
of earth's resounding energy

A simple smile awash
with joy
pure heart
finds home

******

If; Sin

If love was real
there'd be no sin;
we could hold
each other's fears
against a star-filled sky
under canopy
of silken truth

If time stood still
where would we spin?
Out somewhere
in light of day
hide dark under eyes
they could see
the beauty beneath
a willow

If passion words
could find your heart
I'd write a tome
within a tomb
for only us to bear
safe within arms
that never tire
of the work

If wounds were closed
hope would caress
new meaning
washing away
all the sins
of yesterday

******

What I Want Is Irrelevant

Bound by stitches and glue
I've stared at empty stars,
climbed stairs made of gold;
never seen the raveled thread

Someone once told me
keepsakes can come back
to haunt, but there was never
anything tangible I could treasure

So what makes real?

Made of arid vapors
cold compressed air
in tiny slats
an eye slips through

I had love to share
once upon a fairy tale
where evermore
stole my soul;
abides a long history
into foggy morning

So what makes real?

Closed heart
through fragrant blossom
six digits
300 words
too many obstacles
one broken artery
two promises
small hope
and the scent
of the Pacific

as the backdrop
to one kiss
we never shared

******

Broken Trance

Before time, a sullen coil
wrapped itself in shallow
kiln-fire vision
of green palms,
starburst showers
hailed the birth
from my Southern terrace.

Phantom shadow covertly whispers
"I never tasted rainbows mist."
Acrid backlash with strings
dangle about the toes
attached to a worn sole,
but I know my place.

Before time, words bent
like the sea turns its white
into harmonized holiness
and dreams become
the only hope to suspend.

My sixth sense felt the sting
before the tear of parchment
dried the ink in multi-layered
dimensions under glass ruins.

There was never anything here
to love from any distance
only remains of broken seashells
the tourist left behind,
and I know my place.

******

Day

It's just another day
but it's gotten the better
of me, what with mortality
statistics staring me down
daring me to jump
out of the fire
into rings of blue onyx

Six and counting
five wishes
four pieces
three sacred vows
two-handed human
one

it's no secret
I hide in kryptonite
caves laced with silver
alchemist heaven

restoration progresses
on schedule
liftoff momentarily halts
waits for passenger
to skim up the side;
shimmy back into full
throttle position

We land

it's a new day
same as any other

******

Hollowed Haven

Organic Origin:
Weary walk
snake charmer
empty sleeve
full of disgrace
a gravesite
trepidation's hollow

Mystic Misses:
Raspberry kisses
twist 'round
a pinky
in earshot
of someone's
deepest darkest den

Valid Valor:
Did we really think
this through?
With careful weighing
of emotional derailment
quietly swept
into something
it wasn't

as if denying
passion
would somehow
erase what we held

Retrospective Repose:
I see now
it wasn't a one slant;
it was a union
of dialectical deity
and dutiful days

that split the oak
from its core

an opposite reaction
some chemical colloid;
friction flight
unlike fear
and might

Addictive Aphorism:
Still,
in the night
when the moon
hides smite
and dreams are only
drug-induced byways,
there is a play
that comes;
inherent habit
decayed from malnourished
igneous neither recognized
nor grasped

Glacial Grace:
The intangible
enumerates
until dust settles
back into a winter
home where all these
things I put off
to do when I am old
come crashing down

******

November Falls

"It's time"
I hear tiny voice
make its way
into dead wall
where no one can hear

A play on words
trickery and deceit
lie in a warped warehouse
music filters
air singes

bites sinful shame
loss
memory hides
in yesterday

A child runs
free
sits in corners
watching spiders
as they build
then fall
like November

blind side
covets developmental delay
government deplores

all around
under a desk
wait for the all-clear whistle
or was it a bell?

Sit in a lightless room
ink by candle
dot the eyes
with psychedelic symphonies

oh! to go back
and reverse
a process
take wisdom
for granted;
insight for truth
when all along
it is only what
we tell it to be

No matter how you lay
the cards
shuffle, deal, shuffle, deal
they stack
the same as the next
time
the next time
the next time
the next lie

Lunatic phrases
that mean nothing
that mean everything
that mean anything
in between, you can
scratch your way through

It's all a maze
amazing
amazing grace
I can't seem to
pronounce
with clarity
only deprivation clamor

Move on
to watch snow
drift
like November

******

so far

please don't tell me
to ignore my feelings
not when I've come so far
I had too many years of
ignoring what stood right
in front of me, only to find
truth hidden in black and blue
bruises that left resin scars
deep inside

******

White Tea and the Republic

SciFi Reality:
Orwellian moves closer
with each day
I ponder where to be
when the time comes
{selfish veins}

Where is safe?
Which side to take
or fake
to survive?
{bottled water reservoir}

TapDance:
What were those clicks
on long-distance love
heels that forced
lunar speak?
{guarded mystery}

Our privacy closed
years ago;
we just stay blinded
to truth
and shift to imminent
quarters
{matrix revisited}

1978;
a year to imprint
and retain
grey matters
where white purges
into black
to become
haze

{foggy horizon}

Antichrist Hints:
Was my first impression
the one to regard
or one to respect
with trepidation
supplanted by subliminal
sect?
{ousted by operation overpower}

Sodden Trodden:
Fear breeds fear;
knowledge goes a long way
to the primary paranoid province
{suspicious spine}

But
you can only call
a kettle black
after you've sipped
the tea
steeped just so
{stewed sewage}

******

11.08.infinity

She never fell
he never healed
from love they
couldn't master

Friends fall
by the wayside
in chipped calibration

but
this bond
does not bend
nor break
under siege
of deceitful trespasser

Attempt to break the spirit
of a pre-cast foundation
falters

I am not moved
nor stirred
by pickax noises
pictured in pretty
Christian name

A dark woman came to me
in a dream, like a prophet
seeking to calm
the silent whirl

She told me to look
in the eyes, the way
they move over mine;
the way they light
when my name

is aroused
from deep repose
where you try
to forget
all we were

Small comfort
to hold
when winter
creeps ever closer;
never~found closure
emanates harmonious hue

She told me
you never got over me
she told me
I never fell out of love

with the same conviction
that he told me
I never drown

******

Seven Days to Push

Count on fingers
while holding breath
underwater altar
in shattered dream
where white cars
become trash;
the view from the beach
on a hill
backwards
surrealism
traces images
over parchment
in words that fracture
simultaneously

That grin on his face
looks like a child
who just wandered into
a candy store
with a blank check

And we wait
for the inevitable
to come, wash us clean
of sin and war
and famine
that will follow
until we implode
natural occurrence
in line
unbound
glory marching home

******

Three Sides of the Equation

I don't do Math
and if I could
well
you can't go back
anyway
there's no bridge
after you've burned
the ignition switch
that turns

In waiting for the weight
on shoulders to melt
under heat of the pill
that is immune
to a system
long on overdrive

Short on fuse
that stills
the framework
of distorted memories
I didn't make alone

Torn, like a tired cliche
sky full of crescent rain
drops out from clouds
bent on sealing grey
with white-tinged traces
of hope

I know there are layers
he isn't aware of
to see the fine lace
lined beneath
a storm

I switch back and forth
classic rock
to alternative
to classical
smooth the edges
of rough stems
that steams water

******

Empty Float

Knock yourself out;
Insanity rift
sounds inaudible
What am I tuned into?

There's nothing more
to say, to speak
to feel, to walk
What am I doing here?

I don't feel the depth
I don't feel at all
I don't reach

Why do you feel the need
to shout to the world
secrets best left buried?
Is it redemption,
clarity,
a voice to call your own?

I am so full
of empty that
nothing can
penetrate

Anarchy cries
softer
I was raised from the dead
for purpose
that loses itself
in the sheaf

Who crawls here
to read between
lines and scattered

photographs
that do not make a life?

Piece me back
together
with anima mortar

Caress this flesh;
create sin
to wash away
the shoreline
Split the sea
in two rows
to escape

I want to feel
history pages;
keep me from
tears to be shed
on some holier day

******

Secret

I shared my
every name
with you
although
I understand
your need
for secrecy

Cloaked in God
thumping bible quotes
and good wishes
for a sad world
you travel
though the empty zone
of ratified reason

No sacrament broken
in early morn light
I stand only in awe
and half-full coffee cup

******

Gluttony

I'm so erratic
so erratic
irrational
gluttony sweet
inside

inside
along the seams
ravel round red rover red rover
send Christ back over

It's the madness
you want close
next to you,
it's the sadness
you need close
next to you

Repetitive {e}motion
of range 100 percent
CONGRATULATIONS!

Stand back
while she blows
a new hole
in your heart

like a dead seamstress
stitching the unfit

Dump my flesh
while you wear
a new suit and tie;
find your way
among the rich

This so isn't you
the way you are,

who you are
is who I fell in love with

the carefree
spirit
I lost,
I only covet what
I lost

I exist in the backlot
of your soul
like a scratch on your favorite song
on your favorite cd

I argue with God,
beg answers
like it is some sick joke,
some sense of humor

I beg to differ in motivation
but sensory overload
takes control
over heart and reason

And ......
alone in a distant season
I will know
these earthly matters
never mattered anyway

******

My Henry

Do the lies catch up with you
as you steel the late fuel;
crash into an armload of mourning?

I can't do night like that anymore
no stomach for a roller-coaster
that comes
to a dead halt;
sends vacant dreams
only salty air to comfort
these limbs

Maybe Huck is right
about the *comet*
and unlike science,
it just is

Nothing changes
or moves
or fades
or stills

I have to keep in mind
this isn't the verbal version
of "Fight Club"

And while Hugh slept
smugly in the bed,
foolish jaded star
pissed time away
like it was there to spare

It was only delayed
moon storms passing
after all
that will haunt evermore

******

Simple Mode

We cling too long
to past events
and people
who balance
weight of being

And just before
going under
buoy back
to the surface
to survive purgatory

After climbing from hell,
it's a soft place
to create the path
to Nirvana;
to carve a niche
in the foundation
with a gourd

leave crumbs
for the next survivors

******

Dope Soap

I've got pain
for my mantle
soap for my hair
music for lies
where we pretend
we're on the big screen
wielding word slings
for stone

I can't imagine a world
without your grace;
ever-presence
to linger over the pier
watch the sunset
with the same fervor
as fall's eve
yet different with each stroke

of pink and rust shades
that enchant
the house on the hill

it's not for sale anymore
but the grey still is
like a forgotten strip
of land, forsaken for choicer
views

Night comes too soon

214

******

Dead Toes

I thought I could sleep
without
incidence of discreet hello's
and a glance here and there
a smile that keeps secrets

This sweet tea
tops off the night
while the moon
hides in the fog
and trees obscure
a view to forever

I try to find common
ground that binds
and bends
between us,
something to stitch
us in two wholes

Three days
until silent novena
wish results
in more of nothing

Tired awake
wired in rare garment
fashion
a token gesture,
a wave and a goodbye

Quiet quakes await
in the wings of your shoulder
loosen the grip
while I let go
completely

a toast to posterity
a kiss for yesterday

******

TimeTrails

Wait for prairie prayers
to be answered;
{he doesn't want me}
Toil with oils
and watercolors
that swirl
in imagination;
wait only for a gold piece
to procure tools
{he doesn't know me}
Richly inspired
to drape
the words into
picture perfect symmetry;
wait on knees to replace numb
{he doesn't need me}
Severance, reverence
eagerly await
to see what comes next;
I'm almost there
almost ready
{he doesn't love me}

******

As I Need

I can't get enough sleep
and lucid dreams
aren't as clear as I need

Moving floors
and walls that bend
with every movement
soft feet that land in pliable tile

Jump easy as natural
as if we were born into this

Wheelchair driven
from one ex-ray
to a test

And then,
in a familiar place
college that was a town
self-sufficient

with a mall
and stores
and doctors
"I've been here before."
but I knew it was the wrong place
this time

Sun-filled naps
warm face
as skin creeps
into smoother tones
while visions dance

******

Endowment Edifice

Rev up the revolution
{it hasn't come yet}
Seduced by
"What would Jesus drive?"
Money Market Sunday
hip hugger jeans
vicious video games
terrorists
with cancer carrying
cell phones

ghost neighborhoods
where only the hoods dare
go
self-contained communities
where no one comes
out after dark
sheltered in our parents
fears

we were gonna charge
the world

"Latte, Mocha
Verona, Sumatra
or Frappuccino, please?"

Let's stand on end
together
hand in hand
heart to heart
regenerate the earth
as it turns

We assume ourselves
at DisneyWorld

Six Flags
Soak City
but we never get wet

We toil with words
post on boards
that reek of bored sprite

We sip coffee
while reading
wannabe poets

tarot prophets
who only tread
the surface
in quaint coffee shops
that spring up
as if coffee
were an act of Congress

break the laws
of God
and seek lust
to keep warm
on black ice

Flex muscles
tuck tummy's
trim the fat
with high tech
laser beams

We kill ourselves
when we kill
the dirt
pollute the mind
of genius
who are here
to transform
sapient score

Simply stated
no one moves
to close the gap
to heal the flesh
to share the wisdom

It all sounds so good
in a mic
on paper
on streets of tired pavement,
between sheets of parchment,
we peddle poetry
to save the planet

Let's stand
shoulder to shoulder
heel to heel
recover
the land
sever chemical imbalance
we bought
from controlled media
avenged by authority
broken like breach
coddled without care
drugged by dreams

medicate the senses
so we can't see the wool
for the forest
as it burns
in Heaven
or Hell
as it is on Earth

One hundred million
is too hearty to turn away

Silenced by secret storms
we created
while trying to raise standards

we only raise the dead

while waking to the revolution

******

As Streams Run

I cover my tracks
with white baby powder
fresh scent
subtle was never an ideal virtue
to spare or stare
as streams run

Under the gun
inspiration finds its happy
little home
on a shoulder
tiered
carrying
the world
around
in 90 seconds
or somesuch

as it were
bent

Ah! But the joy
of old letters
and poems
gathered on the way
to crease and fold
to have roses
in December

Grey and tortured
arms that weigh
with muscle
torn and rent
upon a desert
to be lent
as winter

creeps in the window

******

Crimson Chasuble

Looking for some
redeeming quality
in ruby satin slippers
fit for running
lace along the edge
of the street
midnight midriff
the strummer
strings a perfect pitch
of G

Down here
we filter
smoke like sewer
rats, slice the vein
with a precise blade
let the juice run
rabid

A dark stutter
walks in
with nothing
but a smile
to pass the next
creature we sliver
inside a hand-carved cave

I want to confess
it's been over thirty
years;
I don't know where
to begin, where to end

What penance would a priest
bestow pagan sinner?

I let it simmer
in the bath
while boiling water
runs over imperfect manicured toes;
green faded teal

Hunger and sleep
remain a mystery
vetoed checks
float
another day

I like the feeling
of communion
with another
flesh to flesh
becoming one
immaculate skin

I need a messiah
to teach
what I lost
what I forge
so easily
I forget;
makes forgiveness
a snap

I am not God
or Goddess
it isn't mine
to remit

******

Frontal

The nearly departed
lay under a table
in the front room
trip over like
red legs that dangle
disturb sleep
make coffee
without noticing
its body
or scent
an omen
to sift
or ignore
the ignorant sign
culprit unknown
intruder among
the enemy

******

It's A Given

The dumbing of America
surpasses ignorant
replies given in
scores of tests
that fall like shadows
in a row of forgotten graves
where we bury soldiers;
fail like safe shelters
in winter

******

On You

You sleep
snug in raw smugness
that doesn't look good
on you
so easy to blame
with an easy target
my past terrors
and sorrows
surface in your mind
to call out the demons
that was a lifetime ago

it's all so familiar
comfort
words
and
wars
battle scars
and badges
you pretend to know me
I pretend to care

like I need a reminder
of fault lines
that crease
with days
and nights like these
you are dead to the world
the quiet undertow
that takes it all in
takes it on the chin

but I don't bite

******

Cookie Cutter

Are we but flesh
our time in this corner
a sunset, a dust storm
light from light
out of dark edges
shaped from one cast
like a stone thrown
into a cold void

******

Away The Night

I dreamed of a deluge
red tears flowed
like a river,
but
it isn't this
that haunts
awake the night
to eradicate
the demons
I possess

Images blur
vague redemption
in a tiered house
with too many rooms
to count, to roam

to remain
ever~elusive
in mind's eye
behind blind vision

crushed black velvet sky
will not stalk

Fragments flash
while entertaining
a new dawn

sleep is for the meek
I no longer dream
my self to keep
memories tweaked
that only play
in tired scheme

Blood flowed
freely, open
on the roads
and in between
no surrender
no relief
no reprieve
no sorrow
no pain

Release
emotion
remiss

I cannot place

******

Race

Shadows play the hall
where stairs meet an open window

There is no seam
to close
no room to seal

No one's fate
is at risk
when you breathe

Chest rises
falls
{relax the round
part of the back
while stretching
hands together
folded in a pattern}
we gather from inference

Legs pound the mattress
restless form
measured in mesmerized
foray

This raging glory
of passion

it burns
fatigue;
different
than before

Cast stones
upon ocean's door

Short steeples
alternate flat roofs;
reside in perfect view

I keep vigil
for a name
to appear
a voice
I recognize
in a lost sea

but
it is I who is
disconnected
from the past
where it all feels
surreal
like watching
a movie of someone
else's life

Memory fails
like a sharp slice
against skin
that bleeds
open wound

cold familiar phase
to snuggle
the moon
until morning
finds reason

******

empty bloated pills

there is but a moment
when we stop
{never a conscious thought}
to take to bed
when dreams play
nightmarish waves
death comes
knowing
there is no fear

tell me something
just out of reach

******

Tongue Depressors

There is a mood
that sweeps quietly
through each string
of who we are

distrust of deconstructed
words, emotions
categorized
long ago

they come to singe
each one of us
in their own manner

like a chameleon
a shade of lipstick;
a generic scent of perfume
giving each its own secret
alchemy in fusion

******

I Need

I need a diamond
that shines from
the same cast

I need a shrink
to wrap cellophane
from trees

I need caffeine
bright and early
to open eyes

I need a rose
soft and pink
to hide in treasure's bosom

I need a place
to land
when the world ravels

I need a man
who understands
without words

I need a poem
that speaks
gentle yet deep

******

Accumulated

I'm not myself
lately
Too much comes
swooping down
to kill
the remains
of the hollow

empty realm
of shattered peace

I break
in pieces
small fragments
that do not fit

I shiver at the slightest
gust of wind that blows
from the north
in hallowed halls
mixed with ocean air

It's been days since
I've been here

Inhale shallow drags
of a madness sinking in
and I fear the worst

Clearly, I don't belong here

I stir in place
like a runner
in water
Isolation tank
for the weary

it's a boatload
of history
about to erupt
under the skin's surface
pinprick the innocent

******

Autonomous Ascension Acceleration

Fallen Friday
from the week
that ends
7-day rush;
commotion -
chaotic motion

The moon sets
soft on petals
of snow
covered in chocolate
fizz

Saturn watches
the bastion
of us all
in awe of civilization
gone awry

Black market clearance;
a security measure
not a beat
or lash to bat
Blast through polka-dot
rhythm

Catch a raindrop
on your tongue
to trade for weapons

The game
the sport
the trivial matter
of commercial success
a holiday to hide

in days to come
we will find a way
to liberty, libation
and love

******

There Lies The Tin Man

Nothing satisfies
simple wet appetite
It's a lie, vowed
to carry to my grave

Strenuous stagger
to stow

Tired of the empty
awareness that lies
blanketed
beneath
a massive vacant tomb

Immobile to alter
the course,
to set up a new altar

I fall to my knees
and accept the lot
of cards
as they are delivered;
I am not

Misguided tears
tell the tale
of a spent life
not ready to go

Angels keep me
once more

It's cold
and hard
like steel
like truth

some deny

Always a personal
missive
no reply
comes

I sleep
in torn
dreams
that forge,
forgive,
and forget
by dawn

by some grace
in a flash
of divinity

a trinity
formed
the shroud
of mysteries
we solve
next time

next time

******

Holiday 46

Christmas comes
another year ends
ignore sounds and scents
this season

Circle dates with cinnamon rings
candy apple smiles
caramel-filled chocolate dreams

******

Leaving

We walk
in opposite directions
share the world
on uneasy shoulders
courageously
take the break
down of the west

******

Where We Stood

I wonder if you can hear me now
so far from the center
where we stood

when we got what we wished
in a blink
yet in another
it all washed away

No new experiments
to take on
no trials too stiff
a penalty
forever

The clock dwindles
down down
it falls
in cycles

This cold California morning
reminds me of Nashville
twenty-something years ago
when Frost never died
under heavy quilt
coffee brewed
as I dreamed
landscapes
that were still attainable

but the road turned
and choices played
their course

It is only selfish youth
that makes nostalgia

a bittersweet potion

The same greed
that binds me in
keeps me
from making peace
with the word

12.26.02

I:
13 blackbirds
on a telephone wire
chatting up the sky
They fly off
one by one

II:
Sure, I must have
heard of Calliope River
somewhere, some time
other than now

III:
This sore forms a soft scab
to leave a small scar;
it's a metaphor
for what is
just under my nose

IV:
Within reach,
we are taken
without grief
or solace

V:
The story
is like Petra;
a dream planted
and haven't I always
seen the lighter side
of two equations
that bring balance?

VI:

248

Three blackbirds return
I hear birdspeak
in high volume
surround-sound
blue screen fade
to heaven

******

when?

when comes the penance?
when comes remorse?
when comes the prophecy?
when comes recourse?

give me back the dreams
I need clarity
open the curtain
I'm ready
{or not, I have to know}

is this like the matrix?
once chosen,
there's no going back

the cogs turn
snap snap
[but not like before]

I need to talk
I need to hear

I push it aside
with fervor
maybe it is not my place
to ascertain

when comes the peace?
when comes the rain?
when comes the prince?
when comes the reign?

******

Run

Did we run out of words
to speak
while the earth
invented new ways
to ignite trepidation?

I burn

a soft, warm comfort
to rationalize misplaced fear

I run

I pray

mixed words
to be disengaged
discharged
in some future
scene

where I know
right is right
and can only stand
in awe of what is
and why

Printed in Great Britain
by Amazon

26815698R00143